WORKBOOK FOR BREATH

Copyright © 2020

All rights reserved. No part of this publication may be reproduced, stored in a retrieval system, or transmitted in any form or by any means (including electronic, mechanical, photocopying, recording, or otherwise) without prior written permission from the publisher.

THIS WORKBOOK BELONGS TO

_____

_____

Personal Reflection

_____
_____
_____
_____
_____
_____
_____

How this chapter(s) made me feel

_____
_____
_____
_____
_____
_____
_____

Things on my mind

_____
_____
_____
_____
_____
_____
_____

Lesson Learnt

Lesson from chapter (s)

_____
_____
_____
_____
_____
_____
_____
_____

I am grateful for

_____
_____
_____
_____
_____
_____
_____
_____

Goals I Envision

_____
_____
_____
_____
_____

Improvements I Seek

_____
_____
_____
_____
_____

My Weekly Plan / Meditation

Monday:

_____

_____

Tuesday:

_____

_____

Wednesday:

_____

_____

Thursday:

_____

_____

Friday:

_____

_____

Saturday:

_____

_____

Sunday:

_____

_____

Personal Reflection

How this chapter(s) made me feel

Things on my mind

Lesson Learnt

Lesson from chapter (s)

_____
_____
_____
_____
_____
_____
_____

I am grateful for

_____
_____
_____
_____
_____
_____
_____

Goals I Envision

_____
_____
_____
_____
_____

Improvements I Seek

_____
_____
_____
_____
_____

My Weekly Plan / Meditation

Monday:

___

Tuesday:

___

Wednesday:

___

Thursday:

___

Friday:

___

Saturday:

___

Sunday:

___

Personal Reflection

How this chapter(s) made me feel

Things on my mind

Lesson Learnt

Lesson from chapter(s)

_____
_____
_____
_____
_____
_____
_____
_____

I am grateful for

_____
_____
_____
_____
_____
_____
_____
_____

Goals I Envision

_____
_____
_____
_____
_____

Improvements I Seek

_____
_____
_____
_____
_____

My Weekly Plan / Meditation

Monday:

___

Tuesday:

___

Wednesday:

___

Thursday:

___

Friday:

___

Saturday:

___

Sunday:

___

Personal Reflection

How this chapter(s) made me feel

Things on my mind

Lesson Learnt

Lesson from chapter (s)

_____
_____
_____
_____
_____
_____
_____
_____

I am grateful for

_____
_____
_____
_____
_____
_____
_____
_____

Goals I Envision

_____
_____
_____
_____

Improvements I Seek

_____
_____
_____
_____

My Weekly Plan / Meditation

Monday:

Tuesday:

Wednesday:

Thursday:

Friday:

Saturday:

Sunday:

Personal Reflection

How this chapter(s) made me feel

Things on my mind

Lesson Learnt

Lesson from chapter(s)

_____
_____
_____
_____
_____
_____
_____
_____

I am grateful for

_____
_____
_____
_____
_____
_____
_____
_____

Goals I Envision

_____
_____
_____
_____

Improvements I Seek

_____
_____
_____
_____
_____

My Weekly Plan / Meditation

Monday:
_____
_____

Tuesday:
_____
_____

Wednesday:
_____
_____

Thursday:
_____
_____

Friday:
_____
_____

Saturday:
_____
_____

Sunday:
_____
_____

Personal Reflection

How this chapter(s) made me feel

Things on my mind

Lesson Learnt

Lesson from chapter (s)

_____
_____
_____
_____
_____
_____
_____

I am grateful for

_____
_____
_____
_____
_____
_____
_____

Goals I Envision

_____
_____
_____
_____
_____

Improvements I Seek

_____
_____
_____
_____
_____

My Weekly Plan / Meditation

Monday:
_____
_____

Tuesday:
_____
_____

Wednesday:
_____
_____

Thursday:
_____
_____

Friday:
_____
_____

Saturday:
_____
_____

Sunday:
_____
_____

Personal Reflection

How this chapter(s) made me feel

Things on my mind

Lesson Learnt

Lesson from chapter (s)

_____
_____
_____
_____
_____
_____
_____

I am grateful for

_____
_____
_____
_____
_____
_____
_____

Goals I Envision

_____
_____
_____
_____
_____

Improvements I Seek

_____
_____
_____
_____
_____

My Weekly Plan / Meditation

Monday:
_____
_____

Tuesday:
_____
_____

Wednesday:
_____
_____

Thursday:
_____
_____

Friday:
_____
_____

Saturday:
_____
_____

Sunday:
_____
_____

Personal Reflection

_____
_____
_____
_____
_____
_____
_____
_____

How this chapter(s) made me feel

_____
_____
_____
_____
_____
_____
_____

Things on my mind

_____
_____
_____
_____
_____
_____
_____

Lesson Learnt

Lesson from chapter(s)

_____
_____
_____
_____
_____
_____
_____
_____

I am grateful for

_____
_____
_____
_____
_____
_____
_____
_____

Goals I Envision

_____
_____
_____
_____
_____

Improvements I Seek

_____
_____
_____
_____
_____

My Weekly Plan / Meditation

Monday:

___

Tuesday:

___

Wednesday:

___

Thursday:

___

Friday:

___

Saturday:

___

Sunday:

___

Personal Reflection

_____
_____
_____
_____
_____
_____
_____

How this chapter(s) made me feel

_____
_____
_____
_____
_____
_____

Things on my mind

_____
_____
_____
_____
_____
_____

Lesson Learnt

Lesson from chapter (s)

_____
_____
_____
_____
_____
_____
_____
_____

I am grateful for

_____
_____
_____
_____
_____
_____
_____
_____

Goals I Envision

_____
_____
_____
_____
_____

Improvements I Seek

_____
_____
_____
_____
_____

My Weekly Plan / Meditation

Monday:

Tuesday:

Wednesday:

Thursday:

Friday:

Saturday:

Sunday:

Personal Reflection

How this chapter(s) made me feel

Things on my mind

Lesson Learnt

Lesson from chapter(s)

_____
_____
_____
_____
_____
_____
_____
_____

I am grateful for

_____
_____
_____
_____
_____
_____
_____
_____

Goals I Envision

_____
_____
_____
_____
_____

Improvements I Seek

_____
_____
_____
_____
_____

My Weekly Plan / Meditation

Monday:

___

Tuesday:

___

Wednesday:

___

Thursday:

___

Friday:

___

Saturday:

___

Sunday:

___

Personal Reflection

How this chapter(s) made me feel

Things on my mind

Lesson Learnt

Lesson from chapter(s)

_____
_____
_____
_____
_____
_____
_____
_____

I am grateful for

_____
_____
_____
_____
_____
_____
_____
_____

Goals I Envision

_____
_____
_____
_____
_____
_____
_____
_____

Improvements I Seek

_____
_____
_____
_____
_____
_____
_____
_____

My Weekly Plan / Meditation

Monday:

Tuesday:

Wednesday:

Thursday:

Friday:

Saturday:

Sunday:

Personal Reflection

_____
_____
_____
_____
_____
_____
_____
_____

How this chapter(s) made me feel

_____
_____
_____
_____
_____
_____
_____

Things on my mind

_____
_____
_____
_____
_____
_____
_____

Lesson Learnt

Lesson from chapter(s)

_____
_____
_____
_____
_____
_____
_____

I am grateful for

_____
_____
_____
_____
_____
_____
_____

Goals I Envision

_____
_____
_____
_____
_____

Improvements I Seek

_____
_____
_____
_____
_____

My Weekly Plan / Meditation

Monday:

___

Tuesday:

___

Wednesday:

___

Thursday:

___

Friday:

___

Saturday:

___

Sunday:

___

Personal Reflection

How this chapter(s) made me feel

Things on my mind

Lesson Learnt

Lesson from chapter (s)

_____
_____
_____
_____
_____
_____
_____
_____

I am grateful for

_____
_____
_____
_____
_____
_____
_____
_____

Goals I Envision

_____
_____
_____
_____
_____
_____

Improvements I Seek

_____
_____
_____
_____
_____
_____

My Weekly Plan / Meditation

Monday:

___

Tuesday:

___

Wednesday:

___

Thursday:

___

Friday:

___

Saturday:

___

Sunday:

___

Personal Reflection

How this chapter(s) made me feel

Things on my mind

Lesson Learnt

Lesson from chapter(s)

_____
_____
_____
_____
_____
_____
_____
_____

I am grateful for

_____
_____
_____
_____
_____
_____
_____
_____

Goals I Envision

_____
_____
_____
_____
_____

Improvements I Seek

_____
_____
_____
_____
_____

My Weekly Plan / Meditation

Monday:

_____
_____

Tuesday:

_____
_____

Wednesday:

_____
_____

Thursday:

_____
_____

Friday:

_____
_____

Saturday:

_____
_____

Sunday:

_____
_____

Personal Reflection

How this chapter(s) made me feel

Things on my mind

Lesson Learnt

Lesson from chapter(s)

_____
_____
_____
_____
_____
_____
_____

I am grateful for

_____
_____
_____
_____
_____
_____
_____

Goals I Envision

_____
_____
_____
_____
_____

Improvements I Seek

_____
_____
_____
_____
_____

My Weekly Plan / Meditation

Monday:
_____
_____

Tuesday:
_____
_____

Wednesday:
_____
_____

Thursday:
_____
_____

Friday:
_____
_____

Saturday:
_____
_____

Sunday:
_____
_____

Personal Reflection

How this chapter(s) made me feel

Things on my mind

Lesson Learnt

Lesson from chapter(s)

I am grateful for

Goals I Envision

Improvements I Seek

My Weekly Plan / Meditation

Monday:

_____

_____

Tuesday:

_____

_____

Wednesday:

_____

_____

Thursday:

_____

_____

Friday:

_____

_____

Saturday:

_____

_____

Sunday:

_____

_____

Personal Reflection

_____
_____
_____
_____
_____
_____
_____

How this chapter(s) made me feel

Things on my mind

Lesson Learnt

Lesson from chapter (s)

_____
_____
_____
_____
_____
_____
_____
_____

I am grateful for

_____
_____
_____
_____
_____
_____
_____
_____

Goals I Envision

_____
_____
_____
_____
_____
_____

Improvements I Seek

_____
_____
_____
_____
_____
_____

My Weekly Plan / Meditation

Monday:
_____
_____

Tuesday:
_____
_____

Wednesday:
_____
_____

Thursday:
_____
_____

Friday:
_____
_____

Saturday:
_____
_____

Sunday:
_____
_____

Personal Reflection

How this chapter(s) made me feel

Things on my mind

Lesson Learnt

Lesson from chapter(s)

_____
_____
_____
_____
_____
_____
_____

I am grateful for

_____
_____
_____
_____
_____
_____
_____

Goals I Envision

_____
_____
_____
_____

Improvements I Seek

_____
_____
_____
_____

My Weekly Plan / Meditation

Monday:
_____
_____

Tuesday:
_____
_____

Wednesday:
_____
_____

Thursday:
_____
_____

Friday:
_____
_____

Saturday:
_____
_____

Sunday:
_____
_____

Personal Reflection

How this chapter(s) made me feel

Things on my mind

Lesson Learnt

Lesson from chapter(s)

_____
_____
_____
_____
_____
_____
_____

I am grateful for

_____
_____
_____
_____
_____
_____
_____

Goals I Envision

_____
_____
_____
_____
_____

Improvements I Seek

_____
_____
_____
_____
_____

My Weekly Plan / Meditation

Monday:

___

Tuesday:

___

Wednesday:

___

Thursday:

___

Friday:

___

Saturday:

___

Sunday:

___

Printed in Great Britain
by Amazon